# OUR WORLD 2

SECOND EDITION • GRAMMAR WORKBOOK

**Series Editors**
Joan Kang Shin
JoAnn (Jodi) Crandall

T0302846



NATIONAL GEOGRAPHIC
LEARNING

Australia • Brazil • Mexico • Singapore • United Kingdom • United States

# Unit 1

## Present progressive, first person plural

| Question | | | | Answer | | | |
|---|---|---|---|---|---|---|---|
| What | are | you | doing? | We**'re** | **reading.** | | *we're = we are* |
| | | | | | **cutting** | yellow paper. | |
| | | | | | **erasing** | the board. | |

Use *we're* verb + *-ing* for actions happening now.

Note that *you* can be used for one person or many people.

## 1 Look and write.

1. 

What are you doing?

We're reading.

2. 

What are you ______________?

We're ______________.

3. 

______________ are you doing?

We're ______________.

## 2 **Look.** Write sentences.

1. 

______________

2. 

______________

3. 

______________

**3 Look and write.** Write questions and answers.

1. 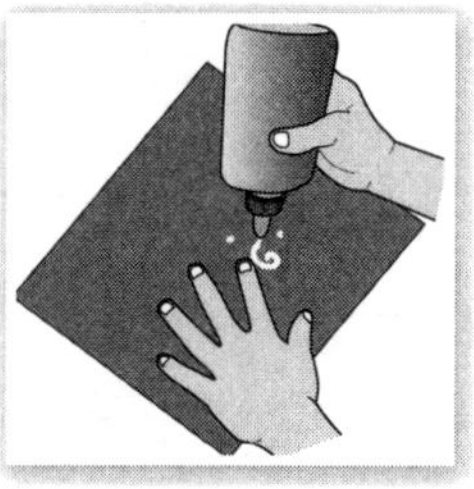

What are you doing ________________________?

________________________________________.

2. 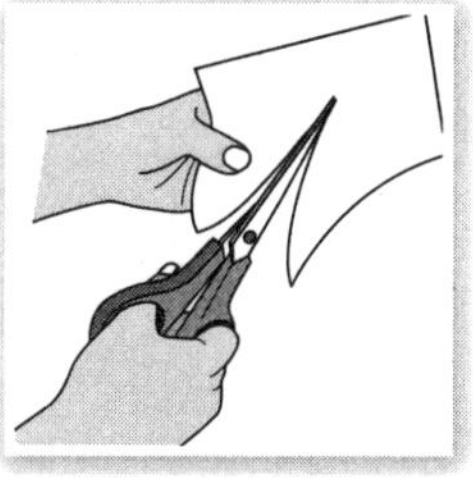

________________________________________?

________________________________________.

3. 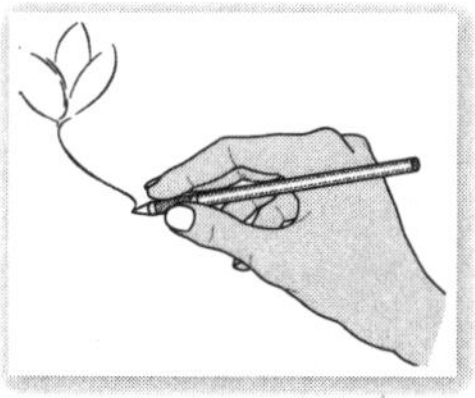

________________________________________?

________________________________________.

**4 Draw and write.** Draw a picture of your class. Write a question and 2 answers.

________________________? ________________________.

________________________.

**Questions with *Are there . . . ?* and short answers**

| Question | | | | Answer | | | |
|---|---|---|---|---|---|---|---|
| **Are** | **there** | any | crayons? | Yes, | **there** | **are**. | *aren't = are not* |
| | | | books? | No, | | **aren't**. | |

Use *Are there . . . ?* questions to ask about more than one thing.

## 1 **Read and match.** Draw a line.

1. Are there any
2. How
3. Are
4. No,
5. Yes,
6. Are there

a. there are.
b. notebooks?
c. there aren't.
d. there any paintbrushes?
e. any markers?
f. many erasers?

## 2 **Read and write.** Think about your classroom.

1. ________________ any pencils on your desk?
________________.
2. ________________ any notebooks in the classroom?
________________.
3. ________________ any erasers on the board?
________________.
4. ________________ any desks in the classroom?
________________.
5. ________________ any balls in the classroom?
________________.

## 3 **Look.** Write questions.

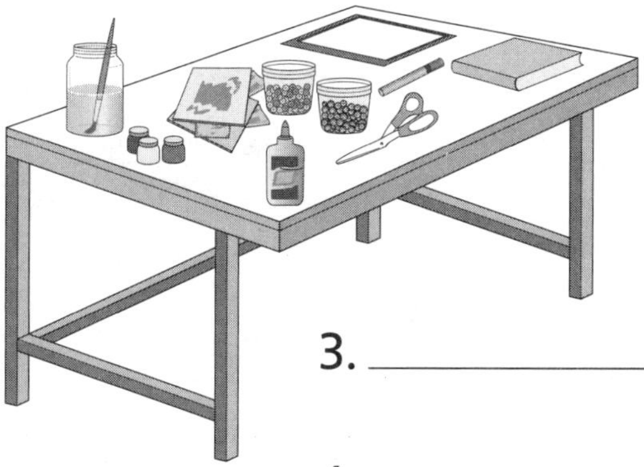

1. Are there any scissors?

2. ______

3. ______

4. ______

## 4 **Write.** Answer the questions in Activity 3.

1. ______ 3. ______

2. ______ 4. ______

## 5 **Look and write.** Ask questions. Then answer them.

1. Are there any paintbrushes? Yes, there are.

2. ______ ______

3. ______ ______

# Unit 2

***What's* + noun + *like* and answers using *It's . . .***

| Question | | | Answer | | |
|---|---|---|---|---|---|
| **What's** | the weather | **like?** | **It's** | windy. | *what's = what is* |
| | | | | cold and snowy. | *it's = it is* |

Ask *What's . . . like?* when you want to know the quality or characteristics of something/someone.

## 1 Read. Circle the word.

1. What day **it's / is** it?
   **It's / Is** Monday.
2. What's the weather **like / do you like**?
   **They're / It's** windy.
3. **What / It's** day is it?
   **It's / They're** Thursday.
4. **How / What's** the weather like?
   **They're / It's** rainy and cloudy.

## 2 Look and write.

1. 
   ________________ the weather like?
   ______________________________________________.
2. 
   What's the weather ______________?
   ______________________________________________.
3. 
   What ______________ the weather like?
   ______________________________________________.
4. 
   ______________ weather like?
   ______________________________________________.

## 3 **Read.** Write sentences.

| S | M | T | W | T | F | S |
|---|---|---|---|---|---|---|
| | Lee's birthday | | Mickey's birthday | | Janie's birthday | Leah's birthday |

1. It's Lee's birthday. ____________? It's Monday.
2. It's Mickey's birthday. ____________? It's Wednesday.
3. It's Janie's birthday. What day is it? ____________.
4. It's Leah's birthday. What day is it? ____________.

## 4 **Look and write.**

1. 

   What's the weather like?

   It's rainy.

2. 

   ____________?

   ____________.

3. 

   ____________?

   ____________.

4. 

   ____________?

   ____________.

## 5 **Write.** Write 3 sentences about today.

____________

____________

**Imperatives**

| | | | | | |
|---|---|---|---|---|---|
| It's rainy. | | **Take off** | your | shoes. | *it's = it is* |
| | | **Put on** | your | boots. | |
| It's sunny. | **Don't** | **forget** | your | sunglasses. | *don't = do not* |

Use the imperative to tell another person what to do.

## 1 **Read and match.** Draw a line.

1. It's rainy.
2. It's hot.
3. It's cold.
4. It's snowy.

a. Put on your coat.
b. Take off your coat.
c. Put on your snow boots.
d. Don't forget your umbrella.

## 2 **Read.** Write a word from the box.

forget off on

1. Take ________________ your sneakers.
2. Don't ________________ your boots.
3. Take ________________ your jacket.
4. Put ________________ your gloves.
5. It's rainy today! Don't ________________ your umbrella.

## 3 Read and write.

1. It's hot. ____Take____ off your boots.
2. It's hot. Don't ________ your bathing suit.
3. It's cold. ________ on your coat.
4. It's rainy. ________ forget your umbrella.

## 4 Look and write.

1.  Don't forget your raincoat.
2. 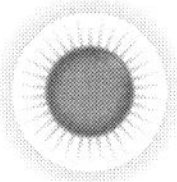 ________.
3.  ________.
4.  ________.

## 5 Draw and write. Finish the picture. Then write 3 sentences.

________.

________.

________.

# Unit 3

***Like* + infinitive**

| | | | | | | |
|---|---|---|---|---|---|---|
| | Do | you | **like** | **to play** | soccer? | Yes, I do./No, I don't. |
| | Does | she | **like** | **to play** | soccer? | Yes, she does./No, she doesn't. |
| What | do | you | **like** | **to do?** | | I like to play soccer. |
| What | does | she | **like** | **to do?** | | She likes to play soccer. |

## 1 **Look and write.** Complete the questions.

1. 

What do they like to do ?

2. 

What do they like ________?

3. 

What do you ________?

4. 

What do they ________?

## 2 **Look and write.** Answer the questions in Activity 1.

1. They like to play basketball.
2. They ________.
3. I ________.
4. They ________.

## 3 Look and write.

1. 

What do they like to do?

They like to play catch.

2. 

______________________________?

______________________________.

3. 

______________________________?

______________________________.

4. 

______________________________?

______________________________.

## 4 Look and write. Ask questions. Write answers that are true for you.

1. 

Do you like to fly a kite?

Yes, I do. It's fun.

2. 

______________________________?

______________________________.

3. 

______________________________?

______________________________.

4. 

______________________________?

______________________________.

**Lot's**

| | | | |
|---|---|---|---|
| **Let's** | watch | a game. | Sure. That sounds fun. ☺ |
| | play | tag. | No, thanks. ☹ |

## 1 Read and circle. Match.

1. Let's bounce a ball.
2. Let's catch a ball.
3. Let's play tag.
4. Let's throw a ball.

a. No, **sure / thanks**. I don't like to catch.

b. **Yes, I do. / Sure**. I like to throw a ball.

c. That sounds like **fun / boring**.

d. Sure. I **like / like to** play tag.

## 2 Look and write.

1. 

Let's bounce a ball.

Sure. I like to play basketball.

2. 

____________________.

OK. That sounds like fun!

3. 

____________________.

No, thanks. It's boring.

4. 

____________________.

OK, sure!

## 3 **Read and write.** What do you think?

1. Let's watch TV. ______________________.
2. Let's play soccer. ______________________.
3. Let's color. ______________________.
4. Let's play tag. ______________________.

## 4 **Look and write.**

1. Let's talk.

   Sure. That sounds like fun!

2. ______________________

   ______________________

3. ______________________

   ______________________

## 5 **Write.** It's Saturday. Write 3 sentences about what to do.

Let's play tag. ______________________.

______________________. ______________________.

# Review: Units 1–3

## 1 **Read and match.** Draw a line.

1. What is it?
2. What do they like to do?
3. What's the weather like?
4. What are you doing?
5. Are there any pencils?
6. Do you like to play baseball?
7. What day is it?

a. It's Saturday.
b. We're cutting.
c. It's snowy.
d. Yes, I do.
e. It's a bathing suit.
f. Yes, there are.
g. They like to jump rope.

## 2 **Look and write.**

1. What are you doing?

______________________

Do you like to cut paper?

______________________

Let's cut flowers.

______________________

2. ______________________

No, there aren't any balls.

______________________

Yes, I do. It's fun.

______________________

I like to play tag.

## 3 Look and write.

1. What's the weather like ________?
It's windy.

2. ________.
Sure. That sounds like fun!

3. ________?
We're flying a kite.

4. ________?
No, I don't. It's boring.

## 4 **Look and write.** Use the words in the box.

| | | | | |
|---|---|---|---|---|
| cold | don't forget | hot | put on | take off |

________
________
________

________
________
________

## 5 **Write.** You and your friends are playing. What's the weather like? What are you doing? What do you want to do? Write 4 sentences.

________
________

# Unit 4

## Prepositions of place

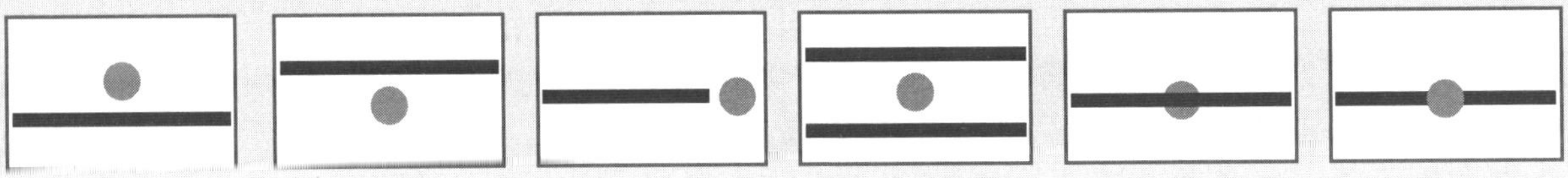

**above** **under** **next to** **between** **behind** **in front of**

Prepositions of place show how two things are related:

*The mirror is above the table.*

## 1 Look and write.

1.  between
2.  ____________
3.  ____________
4.  ____________
5.  ____________
6.  ____________

## 2 Read and draw.

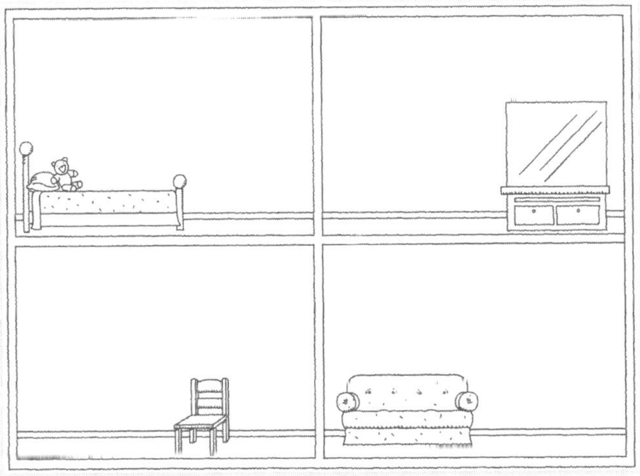

1. The picture is above the sofa.
2. The rug is under the chair in the kitchen.
3. The shower is next to the sink in the bathroom.
4. The stairs are behind the chair in the kitchen.
5. The table is in front of the bed.

## 3 **Look and write.** Complete the sentences.

1. 

The tub is under the shelves.

The shelves are above the tub.

2. 

______________________ the chair.

The chair is ______________________.

3. 

______________________ the bookcase.

The bookcase is ______________________.

4. 

______________________ the stove.

The stove is ______________________.

## 4 **Draw and write.** Draw a room in your house. Write about it.

______________________________________________.

______________________________________________.

______________________________________________.

______________________________________________.

**Subject pronoun agreement: *it, they***

| Question | | | | Answer | | | | |
|---|---|---|---|---|---|---|---|---|
| Where's | | the | **fireplace?** | **It**'s | behind | the | sofa. | *where's = where is* |
| | | | | | in | the | living room. | *it's = it is* |
| Where | are | the | **boots**? | **They**'re | under | the | bed. | *they're = they are* |

Use *where* to ask about location.

## 1 **Write.** Unscramble the dialogues

1. window / is / where / the ______________________________?

   the / is / the / window / above / table ______________________________

   ______________________________.

2. where / chairs / the / are ______________________________?

   room / living / in / the / they're ______________________________

   ______________________________.

## 2 Look and write.

1. 
   Where's the stove ______________________________?
   It's between the door and the sink.
2. 
   ______________________________?
   They're in front of the window.
3. 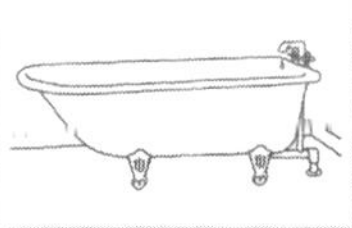
   ______________________________?
   It's next to the sink.
4. 
   ______________________________?
   They're on the bookcase.
5. 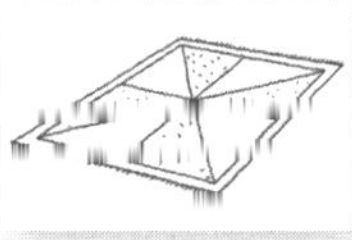
   ______________________________?
   It's under the table.

**3** **Look and write.** Write questions and answers. Use the words.

1. above Where is the window ____________________?
It's above the sofa ____________________.

2. under ____________________?
____________________.

3. between ____________________?
____________________.

4. behind ____________________?
____________________.

5. in front of ____________________?
____________________.

**4** **Write.** Write questions and answers about 3 things in your classroom.

Where's the board? It's under the clock.

____________________

____________________

____________________

# Unit 5

## Telling time

| Question | | | | | Answer | |
|---|---|---|---|---|---|---|
| **What** | **time** | is | it? | | **It's** 11:00 (eleven o'clock). | *it's = it is* |
| **When** | | do | you | get up? | **At** 7:00 (seven o'clock). | |
| | | does | she | | **At** 8:00 (eight o'clock). | |

We often drop *o'clock* when we answer questions about time:

*When do you go to bed? At ten.*

## 1 Read. Circle the word.

1. **What** / **When** does he eat breakfast?
2. What time **is it** / **it's**?
3. **Is it** / **It's** 5:00.
4. When **does** / **do** she play?
5. **When** / **What** do you eat dinner?
6. **It** / **At** 6:00.

## 2 Look and write. Complete the questions about Manuel's day.

1. 

_______________ eat breakfast?

_______________________________.

2. 

_______________ eat dinner?

_______________________________.

3. 

_______________ eat lunch?

_______________________________.

4. 

_______________ play with friends?

_______________________________.

## 3 **Look and write.** Ask questions.

1.  When do you get dressed______________?

2.  ______________________________?

3.  ______________________________?

4.  ______________________________?

## 4 **Write.** Give true answers for Activity 3.

1. ____________________.
3. ____________________.
2. ____________________.
4. ____________________.

## 5 **Write.** Ask and answer about a friend's day.

1. ____________________________? ____________.
2. ____________________________? ____________.
3. ____________________________? ____________.

**Adverbs of frequency**

| Question | | | | | Answer |
|---|---|---|---|---|---|
| What | do | you | do | **every day?** | I **always** brush my teeth. |
| | does | your sister | do | in the evening? | She studies. She **never** watches TV. |

*Always* and *never* come after the subject and before the verb in the sentence:
*I always go to school. She never plays video games.*

## 1 Read and match. Draw a line.

1. What does your sister do on
2. What do you do
3. What does your brother
4. What does your father do in
5. I always

a. every day?
b. the afternoon?
c. Sunday?
d. get dressed before breakfast.
e. do in the evening?

## 2 Read. Circle the words.

1. What do you do **every / in** day?
2. What does your grandfather **never / every day** do?
3. What do you do **every day / always**?
4. I **always play / play always** with my friends.

## 3 Write. Answer the questions about people you know.

1. What does your friend always do in the afternoon?

______________________________.

2. What does your teacher never do?

______________________________.

3. What does your mother never do on Saturday?

______________________________.

**4** **Look and write.** When does Sandra do each activity? Write questions and answers.

| | Monday | Tuesday | Wednesday | Thursday | Friday |
|---|---|---|---|---|---|
| 1. get up at 6:00 | ✓ | ✓ | ✓ | ✓ | ✓ |
| 2. ride a bike | ✗ | ✓ | ✗ | ✗ | ✗ |
| 3. play with trains | ✗ | ✗ | ✗ | ✗ | ✗ |
| 4. go to school | ✓ | ✓ | ✓ | ✓ | ✓ |

1. What does Sandra do every day ____?
   She gets up at 6:00 every day ____.

2. ____________________?
   ____________________.

3. ____________________?
   ____________________.

4. ____________________?
   ____________________.

**5** **Write.** What do you do every day? What do you never do?

____________________

____________________

____________________

# Unit 6

### *How are you?* with answers *I'm* + adjective

| Question | | | Answer | | |
|---|---|---|---|---|---|
| **How** | **are** | **you?** | **I'm**<br>We**'re** | **OK.**<br>**fine.**<br>**great.** | *I'm = I am*<br>*We're = We are* |

### *He/she looks*

| | | |
|---|---|---|
| You **look**<br>He **looks** | **angry.** | No. I'm bored. |
| | **tired.** | Yes. He's busy. |
| | **happy.** | Yes. He's always smiling. |

Answer the question *How are you?* with *I'm* + adjective (*OK, fine, great, so-so*).

## 1 **Write.** Unscramble the sentences.

1. are / you / how ______________________________?
2. look / you / surprised ______________________________.
3. they / worried / look ______________________________.
4. looks / bored / she ______________________________.

## 2 **Read.** Complete the sentences.

1. You __look__ hungry. Yes. __I'm__ hungry.
2. Your mother ________ angry. Yes. ________ angry.
3. Your father ________ bored. Yes. ________ bored.
4. They ________ thirsty. No. ________ hungry.
5. My brother and sister ________ scared. No. ________ surprised.

## 3 Look and write.

1. 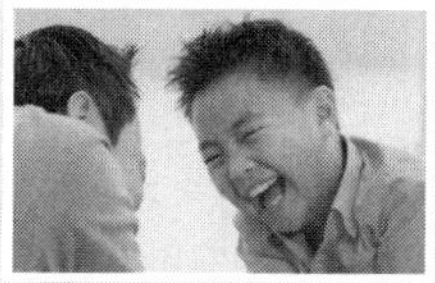 How are you ______?
I'm great ______!

2.  ______?
______.

3. 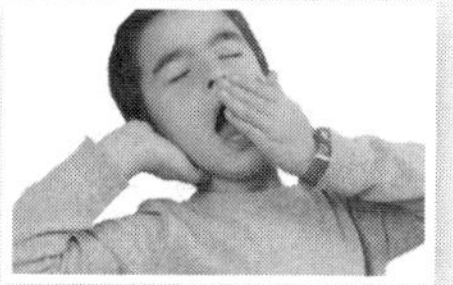 ______?
______.

## 4 Look and write.

1.  **they/scared** They look scared.
No. They're worried.

2.  **you/angry** ______
______

3.  **he/hungry** ______
______

4.  **she/hot** ______
______

## 5 **Draw and write.** Draw a face. Write sentences about how the person feels.

______
______

## Regular and Irregular plurals

| Plural forms | Singular and plural | More examples |
|---|---|---|
| It's my birthday party! Let's cut the cake! The **knives** are next to the **shelves**. | knife → kni**ves**<br>shelf → shel**ves** | tooth → t**ee**th<br>foot → f**ee**t<br>sheep → **sheep** |
| There are some **people** at the party. There are three **men**, three **women**, and five **children**. | person → **people**<br>man → m**e**n<br>woman → wom**e**n<br>child → child**ren** | |
| My **friends** like to play in the park. They like to fly **kites**. | friend → friend**s**<br>kite → kite**s** | |

The regular plural is often formed by adding *s/es* to words, but some plural forms are irregular.

**1 Write.**

1. shelf shelves
2. toys toy
3. tooth ______
4. foot ______
5. people ______
6. sheep ______

**2 Organize.** Write all of the words from Activity 1.

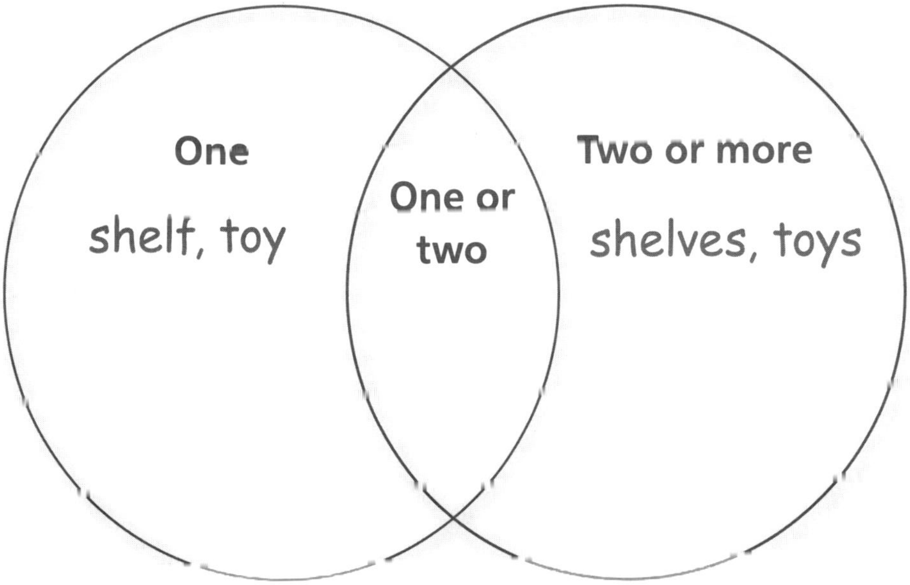

**3** **Read and write.** Rewrite the sentences.

1. The girl is crying. The girls are crying.
2. The person looks angry. ______.
3. The child is yawning. ______.
4. The sheep is sleeping. ______.
5. My foot is under the chair. ______.
6. The baby has one tooth. ______.

**4** **Write.** Use the words. Make sentences.

1. people The people look happy.
2. children ______.
3. teeth ______.
4. shelves ______.

**5** **Look and write.** Write 3 sentences about the picture.

______

______

# Review: Units 4–6

**1** **Read.** Circle the words.

1. The **child** / **children** are in the kitchen.
2. The **person** / **people** are in front of the school.
3. I have two **foot** / **feet**.
4. The **shelf** / **shelves** is above the shower.
5. The window is **behind** / **under** the sofa.
6. The bed is **between** / **next to** the table.

**2** **Read and draw.** Complete the picture.

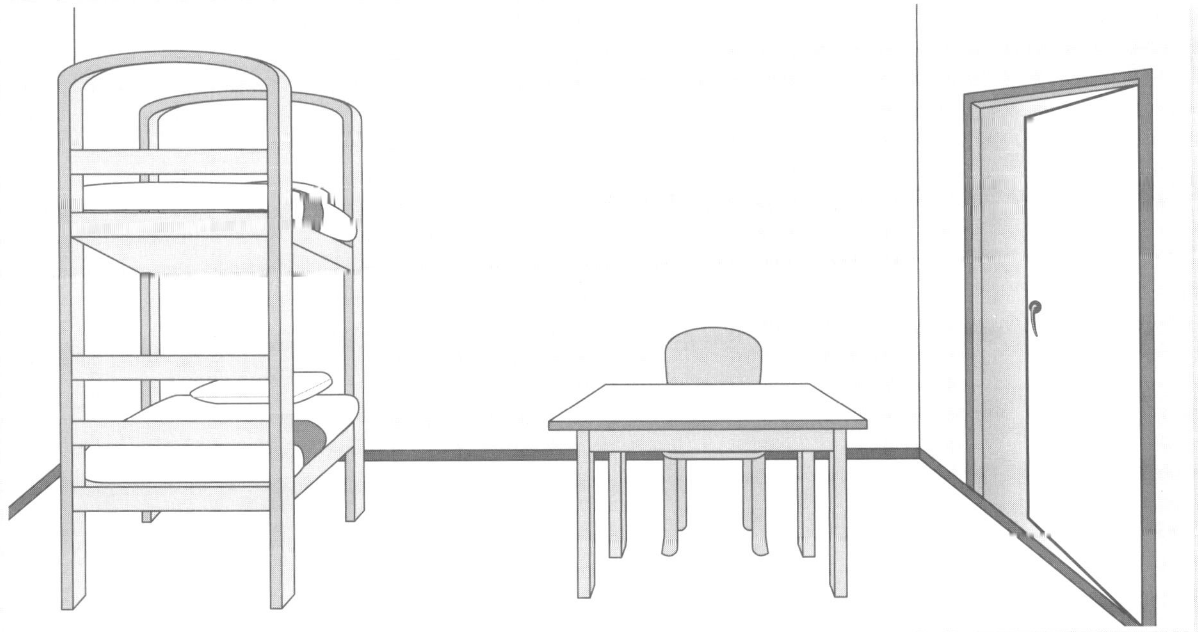

Lisa is in her bedroom. She's next to the bed. There are shelves behind the table. Where are her books? They're on the table. Where is the clock? It's between the table and the door. It's 5:00. Lisa looks hungry.

## 3 Read and write.

1. How are you? ______________________________.

2. What do you always do? ______________________________.

3. What do you never do on Saturday?

______________________________.

## 4 Look and write. Complete the questions.

1. ______________________________?
   The chicken is next to the apples.

2. ______________________________? It's 7:00.

3. ______________________________? We're hungry.

4. ______________________________?
   My parents eat at our house on Saturday evening.

## 5 Look and write. Write 3 sentences for each picture.

1. 
   He's in the kitchen. He always eats breakfast in the morning. He looks hungry.

2. 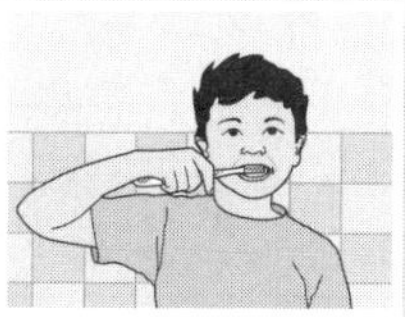
   ______________________________
   ______________________________.

3. 
   ______________________________
   ______________________________.

# Unit 7

**_Can_ and _can't_ for ability**

| | | | | | | | |
|---|---|---|---|---|---|---|---|
| A | penguin | **can** | swim. | It | **can't** | fly. | *can't = can not* |
| Penguins | | | | They | | | |

| Question | | | | Answer | | |
|---|---|---|---|---|---|---|
| **Can** | a | penguin | swim? | Yes, | it | **can.** |
| | | | | No, | | **can't.** |
| **Can** | penguins | | swim? | Yes, | they | **can.** |
| | | | | No, | | **can't.** |

*Can* takes the same form for all persons: *I/you/she/they can run.*

## 1 **Read.** Write *can* or *can't*.

1. A hippo ________ fly.
2. Zebras ________ run.
3. A lion ________ fly.
4. A parrot ________ swim.
5. Penguins ________ fly.
6. A kangaroo ________ hop.

## 2 **Write.** Look at Activity 1. Write about each animal.

1. A hippo can run, but it can't climb.
2. ________________________________.
3. ________________________________.
4. ________________________________.
5. ________________________________.
6. ________________________________.

## 3 Read and write.

1. Can you play baseball?
   Yes, I can ______.
2. Can your friends play soccer?
   ______.
3. Can your grandfather jump rope?
   ______.
4. Can your mother ride a bike?
   ______.
5. Can a baby run?
   ______.
6. Can you and your friends draw?
   ______.

## 4 **Look and write.** Write questions for the answers.

1. 
   Can a lion swing?
   No, it can't.
2. 
   ______?
   Yes, it can.
3. 
   ______?
   No, it can't.
4. 
   ______?
   Yes, it can.

## 5 **Write.** What can you do? Write 3 sentences with *can* or *can't*.

______

______

## Simple present: *Yes/No* questions with *have* and short answers

| Question | | | | | | | Answer | | | |
|---|---|---|---|---|---|---|---|---|---|---|
| **Does** | a | panda | **have** | a | short | tail? | Yes, | it | **does.** | *doesn't = does not* |
| | | | | | long | neck? | No, | | **doesn't.** | |
| **Do** | pandas | | **have** | | short | tails? | Yes, | they | **do.** | *don't = do not* |
| | | | | | long | necks? | No, | | **don't.** | |

The subjects and verbs in a sentence must always be in agreement:
*A giraffe <u>has</u> a long neck. Giraffes <u>have</u> long necks.*

## 1 **Read and match.** Draw a line.

1. Do parrots have colorful feathers?
2. Do monkeys have short tails?
3. Does a giraffe have a long trunk?
4. Does a tiger have sharp teeth?

a. Yes, it does.
b. No, they don't.
c. Yes, they do.
d. No, it doesn't.

## 2 **Read.** Write *do*, *does*, *doesn't*, or *don't*.

1. ____________ an elephant have colorful feathers?

   No, it ____________.

2. ____________ giraffes have long necks?

   Yes, they ____________.

3. ____________ a hippo have big teeth?

   Yes, it ____________.

4. ____________ frogs have long tails?

   No, they ____________.

## 3 Look and write.

1. 

_______________ colorful feathers?

_______________, they _______________.

Can they fly? _______________.

2. 

_______________ sharp claws?

_______________, it _______________.

Can it climb trees? _______________.

3. 

_______________ a long tail?

_______________, it _______________.

Can it jump? _______________.

4. 

_______________ long trunks?

_______________, they _______________.

Can they fly? _______________.

## 4 **Write.** Use the words to write a question. Then answer it.

1. elephants / long trunks

   Do elephants have long trunks? Yes, they do.

2. a tiger / feathers

   _______________

3. a monkey / a long tail

   _______________

4. lions / big teeth

   _______________

# Unit 8

## Simple present: *Wh* questions and answers

<table>
<tr><th colspan="4">Question</th><th>Answer</th><th></th></tr>
<tr><td rowspan="3">What</td><td rowspan="2">does</td><td>your sister</td><td rowspan="2">do?</td><td>She's a vet.</td><td rowspan="6">she's = she is<br>he's = he is<br>they're = they are</td></tr>
<tr><td>his uncle</td><td>He's a firefighter.</td></tr>
<tr><td>do</td><td>your parents</td><td>do?</td><td>They're office workers.</td></tr>
<tr><td rowspan="3">Where</td><td rowspan="2">does</td><td>your sister</td><td rowspan="2">work?</td><td>She works in an animal hospital.</td></tr>
<tr><td>his uncle</td><td>He works in a firehouse.</td></tr>
<tr><td>do</td><td>your parents</td><td>work?</td><td>They work in an office.</td></tr>
</table>

Use *do* as the main verb to ask about a person's job: *What do your parents do?*

## 1 **Read and match.** Draw a line.

1. My father is a chef.
2. My uncle is a doctor.
3. My aunt is a nurse.
4. My grandfather is a vet.
5. My mother is a bus driver.

a. He works in a hospital.
b. She works on a bus.
c. He works in an animal hospital.
d. He works in a kitchen.
e. She works in a hospital.

## 2 **Read and write.**

1. What ______ your aunt do? ______ a firefighter.
2. What does your father ______? ______ a police officer.
3. What ______ your brother and sister ______? ______ farmers.
4. Where ______ your father work? He ______ at home.
5. Where does your sister ______? She ______ on a farm.

## 3 **Read.** Write questions.

1. ______________________________? My brother is a singer.
2. ______________________________? My mother is a teacher.
3. ______________________________? My father works on a train.
4. ______________________________? My grandparents work in a kitchen.

## 4 **Look and write.**

1. 

What does she do? ______________________.

Where does she work? ______________ a kitchen.

2. 

What does he do? ______________________.

Where does he work? ______________ an animal hospital.

3. 

What does she do? ______________________.

Where does she work? ______________ a hospital.

4. 

What do they do? ______________________.

Where do they work? ______________ the city.

## 5 **Write.** What do your parents do? Where do they work? Write about one or both parents.

______________________________________________________________

______________________________________________________________

### Simple present with *want* + infinitive

| Question | | | | | Answer |
|---|---|---|---|---|---|
| What | do | you | **want** | **to be**? | I **want to be** a police officer. |
| | does | your brother | | | He **wants to be** a scientist. |
| | do | your cousins | | | They **want to be** movie stars. |

Use the verb *want* + *to be* to ask about a future job.

## 1 **Read and match.** Draw a line.

1. She likes to sing.
2. My brother plays soccer every day.
3. My sister likes to draw plants and flowers.
4. They can make new things very well.
5. He likes animals.
6. They like to study animals.

a. He wants to be a vet.
b. She wants to be an artist.
c. She wants to be a rock star.
d. They want to be scientists.
e. He wants to be a soccer player.
f. They want to be inventors.

## 2 **Read.** Circle the words.

1. What **do** / **does** you want to be?
   I **want** / **wants** to be an inventor.
2. What do your friends **want** / **wants** to be?
   They **want** / **wants** to be singers.
3. What **do** / **does** he want to be?
   He **want** / **wants** to be an artist.
4. What does your aunt **want** / **wants** to be?
   She wants **to be** / **being** a police officer.

## 3 Look and write.

1.  What do you want to be?

   ______________________________________________.

2.  What do your brother and sister want to be?

   ______________________________________________.

3.  What does your aunt want to be?

   ______________________________________________.

## 4 **Look.** Write questions and answers with *want to be*.

1.  you ______________________________________________?

   ______________________________________________.

2.  your brother ______________________________________________?

   ______________________________________________.

3.  your friend ______________________________________________?

   ______________________________________________.

## 5 **Write.** What do your friends want to be? Write 2 questions and answers.

What do you want to be, Scott?

I want to be a movie star.

______________________________________________

______________________________________________

______________________________________________

______________________________________________

# Unit 9

## Questions and answers with *any*

| Question | | | | Answer | | | | | |
|---|---|---|---|---|---|---|---|---|---|
| Is | there | **any** | meat? | Yes, | there | is. | | | *isn't = is not* |
| | | | pasta? | No, | there | isn't | **any** | pasta. | |
| Are | there | **any** | tomatoes? | Yes, | there | are. | | | *aren't = are not* |
| | | | peppers? | No, | there | aren't | **any** | peppers. | |

*There isn't any pasta = There is no pasta.*

## 1 Read. Circle the words.

1. **Are** / **Is** there any carrots? Yes, there **are** / **any**.
2. Is there **any** / **a** ice cream? No, there **isn't** / **aren't** any ice cream.
3. **Are** / **Is** there any tea? Yes, there **any** / **is**.
4. Are there any **mango** / **mangoes**? **Yes** / **No**, there are 3 mangoes.
5. Are there any **noodle** / **noodles**? No, there aren't **noodle** / **any noodles**.
6. Is there **any** / **a** water? No, there **isn't** / **aren't** any water.

## 2 Read and write.

1. Are there ___any___ potatoes? No, there aren't ___any___.
2. Is there ________ meat? Yes, there ________.
3. ________ there any beans? No, there ________ any.
4. ________________ tomatoes? Yes, ________________.
5. ________________ bread? No, ________________.
6. ________________ corn? Yes, ________________.

**3** **Look.** Write questions and answers.

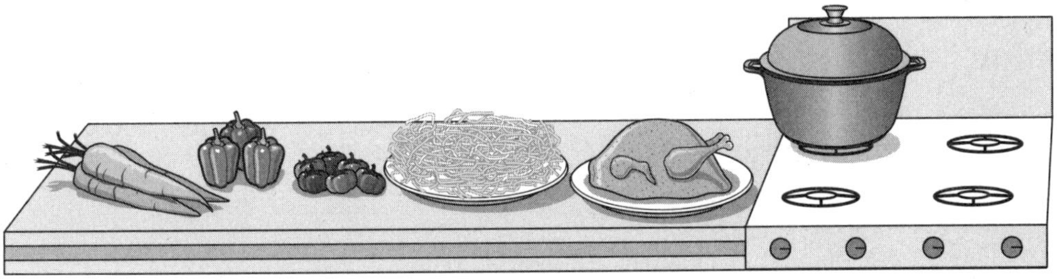

1. ice cream Is there any ice cream ?
No, there isn't any ice cream .

2. tomatoes ______________________________?
______________________________.

3. bread ______________________________?
______________________________.

4. chicken ______________________________?
______________________________.

5. lemonade ______________________________?
______________________________.

6. cookies ______________________________?
______________________________.

**4** **Draw and write.** Draw a picture of your dinner. Write 2 questions and answers.

______________________________

______________________________

______________________________

______________________________

**Polite requests with *may***

| Question | | | | | Answer |
|---|---|---|---|---|---|
| **May** | **I** | have | some | yogurt? | Not now. Dinner is at 6:00. |
| | | | | | Yes. Sure. |

Use *May I . . .* to make a polite request.

## 1 Read. Circle the word.

1. May I have **some** / **any** grapes?
2. **May** / **Is there** I have some yogurt, please?
3. **Yes** / **No**. Sure.
4. **Yes** / **No**. Not right now.
5. May we have some nuts, **thanks** / **please**?
6. May I have **some** / **any** meat?

## 2 Read and write. Find the mistake. Correct the question.

1. I have some may bread, please?

   May I have some bread, please ______?

2. May we some ice cream have, please?

   ______?

3. We may some yogurt have, please?

   ______?

4. May I have grapes some, please?

   ______?

5. We may have some nuts, please?

   ______?

## 3 Look and write.

1. 

May I have some noodles, please?

Yes, here you are.

2. 

3. 

4. 

5. 

6. 

## 4 Draw and write.

**Draw and write.** You want to eat, but it's not time for dinner. Draw a comic. Ask your parents for something to eat. What do they say?

# Review: Units 7–9

## 1 **Read and match.** Circle the words. Draw a line.

1. **Can** / **Do** a turtle swim?
2. **Do** / **Does** a giraffe have long legs?
3. What **do** / **does** your father do?
4. What do you **want to be** / **are** one day?
5. **Do** / **May** I have some nuts, please?

a. He **works** / **is** at home.
b. I **want** / **wants** to be a baseball player.
c. Yes, it **do** / **can**.
d. **No** / **Yes**, not right now.
e. Yes, it **do** / **does**.

## 2 **Look and write.** Use all of the words.

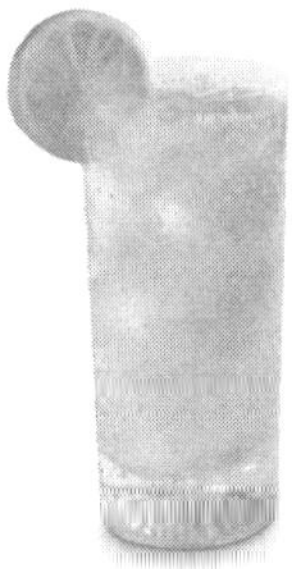

~~beans~~ bread lemonade peppers tomatoes

1. Are there any beans? No, there aren't any beans.
2. ____________________? ____________________.
3. ____________________? ____________________.
4. ____________________? ____________________.
5. ____________________? ____________________.

**3** **Look and write.** Use *can* and *have*.

1.  ______________________________? (long trunks)

______________________________.

2.  ______________________________? (long legs)

______________________________.

3.  ______________________________? (swim)

______________________________.

4.  ______________________________? (fly)

______________________________.

**4** **Look and write.** Write a dialogue. Use *may*.

______________________________?

______________________________.

______________________________?

______________________________.

**5** **Write.** Complete the questions. Then answer them.

1. ______________ your father do?

______________________________

2. ______________ your friend's mother work?

______________________________

3. What do you ______________ one day?

______________________________

# Review: Units 1–9

## 1 Read and match. Draw a line.

1. Let's eat ice cream.
2. It's rainy.
3. He looks angry.
4. What is she doing?
5. Where is the bathroom?
6. May I have my bathing suit, please?

a. No, he's tired.
b. She's drawing.
c. Sorry. We don't have any ice cream.
d. It's behind the stairs.
e. Sure, here you are.
f. Don't forget your umbrella.

## 2 Write.

1. mothers mother
2. gloves ______
3. teeth ______
4. feet ______
5. people ______
6. shelves ______

## 3 Read and write.

1. ______ you swim? ______ can't.
2. ______ you like to play soccer? Yes, ______.
3. What ______ you do every day? I ______ watch TV.
4. What ______ your father do? ______ teacher.
5. What do you ______ do? ______ ride a bike.
6. Where ______ you? ______. I'm cooking.

**4** **Read and write.** Circle the words. Then write your own answer to the question.

1. What **do / doing** you want to be one day? I want to **be / do** a vet.
   I want to be a police officer.
2. What are you **do / doing**? We're **eat / eating**.
   ______________________________________.
3. Where **does / doing** your father work? He **is / works** at home.
   ______________________________________.
4. What do you like to **doing / do**? I like to **cook / cooking**.
   ______________________________________.

**5** **Write.** Ask questions.

1. ______________________? No, a zebra can't fly.
2. ______________________? Yes, kangaroos have long tails.
3. ______________________? Yes, penguins can swim.

**6** **Look and write.** What does your friend do on Saturday? Write sentences. Use the words.

1.  afternoon ______________________________________
   ______________________________________.
2. 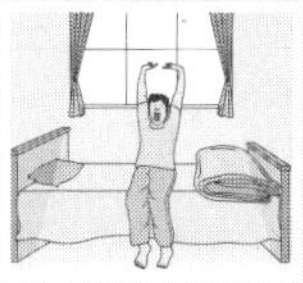 always ______________________________________
   ______________________________________.
3.  never ______________________________________
   ______________________________________.

**7** **Draw and write.** Imagine you're at home. Answer the questions. Then draw a picture.

1. What's the weather like?

   ______________________.

2. Where are you?

   ______________________.

3. What are you doing?

   ______________________.

4. How are you?

   ______________________.

5. What time is it?

   ______________________.

**8** **Look and write.** Use the words. Write 2–3 sentences.

1. 

   cold forget put on

   ______________________________________

   ______________________________________.

2. 

   let's like fun

   ______________________________________

   ______________________________________.

3. 

   may have here

   ______________________________________

   ______________________________________.

## GAME

**Complete the sentences.** Write the words in the puzzle.

**Across**

2. The picture is ________ the bookcase. The bookcase is under the picture.
6. Are there ________ potatoes?
8. My father ________ a kitchen. He's a chef.
10. ________ bounce the ball! Sure, that sounds like fun.
11. The stove is behind the refrigerator. The refrigerator is ________ the stove.
12. What's the weather ________? It's windy.

**Down**

1. ________ an elephant have a long trunk? Yes, it does.
3. Monday is ________ Sunday and Tuesday.
4. A lion ________ swing from a tree.
5. ________ do you get up?
7. ________ you? I'm great.
9. He ________ surprised.